Thank you for your support! Talia
—Khalasya L.

To The Mountains We Go!

Published by VisionWorks

This book is a work of fiction.

Places, events, and situations in this story are purely fictional.

Any resemblance to actual persons living or dead is coincidental.

Library of Congress Catalog-in-Publication Data

Copyright 2022 by Kalashja Womic.

Under penalty of existing United States of
America copyright laws, no portion of this book
may be copied, published, distributed, reprinted,
or otherwise utilized without
express written consent of the author.

All Rights Reserved

Illustrations copyright © 2022

by Kalashja Womic.

TO THE MOUNTAINS WE GO!

By Kalashja Womic

p.cm.

ISBN-13: 978-1-7369008-3-3

Printed in the United States of America

To order additional copies of To The Mountains We Go!

Contact the author at

kalashjal.author@gmail.com

Dedication

This book is dedicated to all girls and boys who never experienced a trip to the mountains. Remember the sky is the limit!

I also went hiking in the mountains. I love to see the green trees and wild red berries.

I finished hiking and now it is time to get rest.

The next morning after breakfast I went fishing. The lake is beautiful. I hope I catch a fish!

Later in the evening I decided to sit by the campfire.
I can hear the crickets chirping.
WOW!

One more night of rest.
We leave for home in the morning.
I am sad, but I had the best time of my life!

THE END!

The Beauty of the
Mountains
I hope you enjoyed
"To The Mountains We Go!"

Remember
"Your destination only stops
when you do!"

Acknowledgments

I would like first to acknowledge God, who helped me on my journey to write my first book. I also want to thank my mom and dad, who pushes me to follow my dreams. I am so grateful for my Grandma "Candy," who supports me every step of the way. I am blessed to have my younger brother, Tre'mars, who "keeps me on my toes!" Lastly, I appreciate "PC" a.k.a. Pastor Cynt. for challenging me to do everything in a spirit of excellence. I truly know the meaning of
"My Pen Is My Friend!"

To The Mountains We Go!

To Contact Author
Please email:
kalashjaL.author@gmail.com

Made in the USA
Middletown, DE
07 November 2022

14368129R00018